REACHING FOR THE STARS

CHRIS BURKE
STAR OF *LIFE GOES ON*

Written By: Bob Italia

Published by Abdo & Daughters, 6535 Cecilia Circle, Edina, Minnesota 55439.

Library bound edition distributed by Rockbottom Books,
Pentagon Tower, P.O. Box 36036, Minneapolis, Minnesota 55435.

Copyright © 1992 by Abdo Consulting Group, Inc. Pentagon Tower, P.O. Box 36036, Minneapolis, Minnesota 55435. International copyrights reserved in all countries. No part of this book may be reproduced in any form without written permission from the publisher.

Printed in the United States.

Cover photo: Archive Photos
Inside photos: Archive Photos 4 & 20
                  Globe Photos, Inc. 7,13, 15, 18, 22, 25, 27, 28 & 30

Edited by: Rosemary Wallner

Italia, Robert, 1955-
    Chris Burke / written by Bob Italia ; [edited by Rosemary Wallner].
    p.   cm. -- (Reaching for the Stars)
    Summary: Examines the life of a young man with Down syndrome who fulfilled his dream of becoming a television star.
ISBN: 1-56239-143-7 (lib. bdg.)
1. Burke, Chris, 1965-   -- Juvenile literature. 2. Life goes on (Television program) -- Juvenile literature. 3. Handicapped in television -- Juvenile literature. 4. Television actors and actresses -- United States -- Biography -- Juvenile literature. [1. Burke, Chris, 1965- . 2. Actors and actresses. 3. Down syndrome. 4. Mentally handicapped.] I. Title. II. Series.
PN2287.B79I85 1992   92-16037
    [B]

International Standard Book Number:
1-56239-143-7

Library of Congress Catalog Card Number:
92-16037

TABLE OF CONTENTS

Life Goes On In a Big Way 5

Born With a Disability 6

Battling The Disability 9

A Boy With a Dream 11

Chris's Big Break 16

"Life Goes On" 19

A True American Hero 28

Chris Burke's Address 32

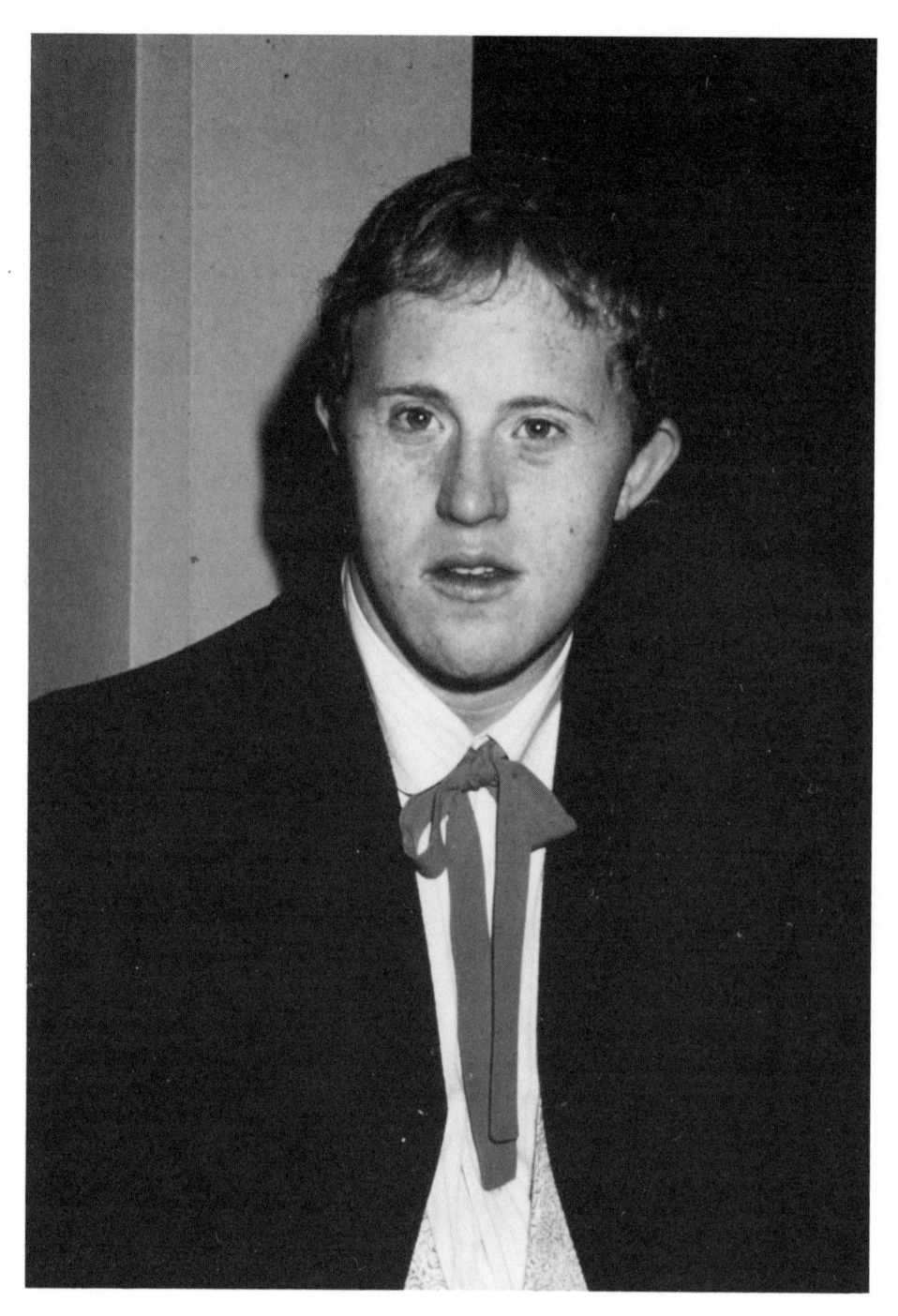

Chris Burke has become a true American hero.

LIFE GOES ON IN A BIG WAY

A doctor took a close look at Chris Burke when he was born and recommended that his parents send him to an institution for the rest of his life. His brother told him to forget his dream of becoming an actor. After he finished school, the only job he could get was operating an elevator. But he never gave up his dream despite his disability. And now, not only has Chris Burke become the first actor with Down syndrome to star on TV, he has become a true American hero.

BORN WITH A DISABILITY

On August 26, 1965, thirty-nine-year-old Marian Burke gave birth to her second son, Chris. Marian and her husband, Frank, a New York City police inspector, had every reason to be happy. Their first three children, Ellen, Anne, and J.R., were healthy children. They even got jobs as child actors and models.

But a few hours after Chris was born, the doctor came into Marian's room with a sad look on his face.

"Your son is a mongoloid," he said. That meant Chris would be retarded. The doctor said that Chris probably would never be able to read, and he wouldn't be able to feed himself. "You should probably consider institutionalizing him right away," the doctor added, "*before* you get too attached."
Marian and Frank didn't listen to their doctor.

Chris with his mother and father, Marian and Frank.

They decided to bring Chris home and care for him.

"There was no way we could have institutionalized him," said Marian. "From the moment we saw Chris, we could not have let him go."

But gradually the disability began to show itself. (Chris's disability is called "Down syndrome." It is named after British physician John Langdon Down, and it affects one out of every 1,000 babies born in the United States.)

Chris didn't speak until he was eighteen months old. When he did, his speech was slow and hard to understand. And it wasn't until he was two years old that Chris took his first steps.

BATTLING THE DISABILITY

The Burke's did all they could for Chris. His sisters, Anne and Ellen, sat with young Chris in front of a mirror and played a game that helped him learn words. They said a word like "eyes," then moved Chris's hand to his eyes. They did this with his nose, ears, and mouth. When he got a word right, they clapped their hands and cheered. The more they cheered, the better Chris did.

J.R. did his part, too. He taught Chris how to swim, and was very patient with him when they played a game of catch. J.R. even took Chris along when he played basketball. He encouraged Chris to dribble and shoot the basketball all by himself. These sporting activities developed Chris's coordination.

"My parents didn't tell us Chris was retarded until he was six months old," said J.R. "It wasn't, 'Gee, isn't that sad,' because it's impossible to be sad around that kid, he has such a great attitude."

When Chris was four years old, his parents enrolled him in New York's Kennedy Child Study Center. There he worked on his reading and spelling skills.

One morning while at home, Chris took a box of Cheerios to his mother and said, "Look, here's my name." Then he picked out the letters C-H-R-I-S from the cereal box. When he was five years old, Chris could write his name.

A BOY WITH A DREAM

When Chris was eight years old, he found a box of old photographs of his brother and sisters when they were child models and actors. The photographs amazed Chris.

"I want to do that!" he announced to his family. "I want to be on TV too!"

Marian didn't know what to say. She never liked to tell Chris that he couldn't do anything. But she didn't want to encourage him to attempt something at which he would fail. Finally, she replied, "I don't know if there would be any parts available for you, dear."

Chris just smiled and said, "Well, you never know."

To prepare himself for his acting career, Chris spent much time at home and at school singing his favorite songs. He also practiced dancing. Chris's determination to become an actor began paying off. He got a part in the school's Christmas pageant, playing a shepherd. He spoke his one line without a mistake. Afterward, he was more determined than ever to become an actor.

Chris finished with his special schooling when he was twenty-one years old. Now it was time to find a regular job. But though Chris was a talented and determined young man, he met with much disappointment. No one, it seemed, wanted to hire a mentally disabled person.

Chris eventually worked in a workshop. He put small items into boxes and sealed them.

But this work was terribly boring, and Chris quit after two weeks.

His sisters found him a job at New York's Public School #138, a school for severely disabled children.

When he was very young, Chris decided he wanted to be an actor.

There he worked as an elevator operator. Though he was happier working at the public school, Chris still wanted to go to Hollywood and become an actor. He saved up $300 for publicity photos and took acting classes at night.

But J.R. did not want to see his brother chase a dream that could not be realized. "Chris," J.R. said one day, "you've got to forget this Hollywood stuff. It's never going to happen."

Chris refused to give up. He knew it could happen. It already had for another actor with Down syndrome.

When Chris was nineteen years old, he saw an episode of the TV show *The Fall Guy* that featured Jason Kingsley, a ten-year-old actor who also had Down syndrome. Chris wrote to Jason. Jason's mother, Emily Perl Kingsley, responded with an encouraging letter. Eventually, the Burkes and the Kingsleys met.

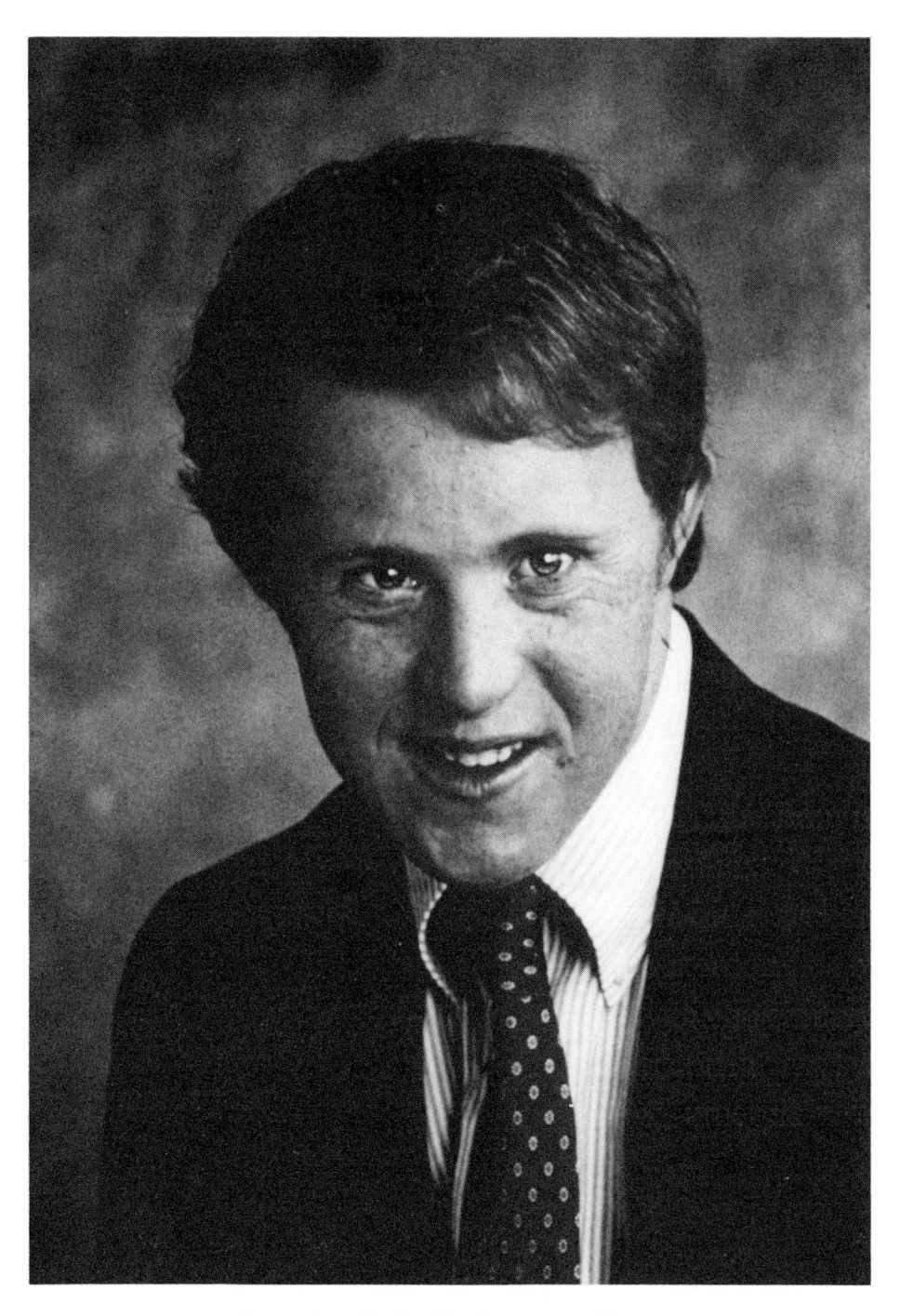

*Even when his family discouraged him,
Chris never gave up his dream of becoming an actor.*

CHRIS'S BIG BREAK

A few years later, TV producer Michael Braverman asked Mrs. Kingsley to recommend an actor with Down syndrome for a TV movie. The movie, titled *Desperate*, would be the pilot for a new television series. Mrs. Kingsley remembered how talented Chris was and recommended him to Braverman.

A few days later, a casting executive in Hollywood called the Burkes. Marian answered the phone.

"Would Chris be interested in an audition?" said the casting executive.

"Let me ask him," Marian replied. Then she looked at Chris. "Christopher," she said, "this lady wants to know if you would like to try out for a part in a movie for television."

Chris was stunned. "Yes, yes, yes!" he hollered. "I'm gonna be in a movie. Ha! A *movie!*"

The studio flew Chris and his father to Los Angeles for the audition with Braverman. When they arrived, Frank Burke decided to let his son face Braverman by himself—to show Braverman how capable Chris was. Chris impressed Braverman.

When the audition was over, Braverman said to Chris, "You've got the part." Chris jumped for joy.

The movie was filmed in Key West, Florida. Chris shared the spotlight with the movie's star, John Savage. It was a dream come true for Chris. The movie aired on ABC in September 1987. But the network decided not to develop the planned TV series.

Chris returned home to his job at Public School #138. He was disappointed, but not broken. He knew one day he would return to Hollywood.

*After starring in a TV movie,
Chris returned home to wait for his next big break.*

"LIFE GOES ON"

While Chris was working in New York, Braverman was working in Hollywood, trying to sell a new series to ABC. The ABC executives hadn't forgotten Chris's performance.

"He's completely charming," said one executive to Braverman. "He jumps off the screen. Do you think you could make a series for *him?*"

Braverman went back to work, recreating the new series around Chris. It would be about a family, the Thachers, who have an older son with Down syndrome. The show would be called *Life Goes On*.

Life Goes On was created to showcase Chris Burke's acting talent.

Said Braverman: "We wanted to show what someone with a disability is capable of."

It took Braverman over eight months to complete the new plans for the series. Finally, Braverman called Chris to Hollywood to film the first show.

Though they were excited about the show, Braverman and the ABC executives had their worries. Chris would have many lines to memorize—forty pages of script per week. And the work would be exhausting—fifteen hours a day. Could he really do it?

Chris, who reads at a fifth grade level, answered those doubts in the first show. His character, Corky, is accused of copying the first stanza of Edgar Allan Poe's poem "The Raven" during an exam. To prove that he knows the poem, Corky must recite the first stanza.

Braverman wanted Chris to read the poem from cue cards. But Chris decided to memorize the poem to show everyone he could handle the work.

Chris Burke, Kellie Martin, Michael Braverman, Bill Smitrovich, and Patti LuPone.

When the scene was filmed, and Chris recited his lines perfectly, the entire cast and crew applauded loudly. Chris had proven himself, and ABC approved the series for its Sunday night schedule.

Life Goes On first appeared on September 12, 1989 (the show also stars Patti LuPone and Bill Smitrovich, Burke's TV mom and dad, and Kellie Martin, his TV sister). TV critics loved the show. And so did America.

Disabled people everywhere found a new hero in Chris Burke.

"*Life Goes On* could have been modeled after my own family," said Marian Burke. "Many of the problems faced by the Thacher family are similar to those we've encountered over the years. To my mind, the show's premise—that love, understanding, patience and, above all, humor, go a long way toward helping a family with a Down syndrome child cope—is right on."

"This show is a miracle," said Emily Perl Kingsley. "We're starving for this kind of realistic production. I hope it blows stereotypes of the disabled out of the water. It's so important to let Chris be himself: appealing, sexy, a real person and not just someone with a label."

Though Chris is a success, the work is still hard. He lives in a comfortable two-bedroom apartment with his father near the Warner Brothers studios. Frank goes to the set each morning with Chris, and helps him with his lines at night.

Most of Chris's scenes are filmed one line at a time. And the lines are kept short. He also has a dialogue coach to help him with his speech and memorization. Since Chris tires easily, most of the important work is done in the morning.

"He used to get upset with himself when he missed a line," said Frank. "He didn't want to waste the others' time. Now he says we'll try again."

Chris Burke, Kellie Martin, and Monique Lanier.

"The only thing that gets him," said Bill Smitrovich, his co-star, "is sharp criticism. So we have all learned not to do that—not with Chris, not with each other."

"I want to be a professional," said Chris. "I want to be like my TV father. He's an easy, calm actor. I don't want to freak out."

Braverman has nothing but praise for his star actor. "Chris has charm and wit and all these great attributes that separate him from so many other people, including many . . . actors. He's extremely high-functioning. He remembers his lines and hits his mark."

Chris Burke and Kellie Martin.

A TRUE AMERICAN HERO

Now that he is a star, Chris Burke uses his fame to help other disabled people. The White House invited Chris to make a public service announcement with President George Bush, telling America about the overlooked abilities of the disabled. And Chris appears at many events honoring the disabled. He even refuses to look at his syndrome as bad.

"I have a slight case of Down syndrome," he said. "I call it Up syndrome."

Chris was invited to the White House to make a public service announcement with President George Bush.

"What impresses me the most about Chris is not what he has achieved, but rather his attitude about life," said Marian Burke. "He is able to find something to smile at or feel good about in almost every situation. He is aware that he's 'different,' but he has never expressed any bitterness about it. In fact, he has a terrific self-image."

Recently, Chris became a spokesperson for the National Down Syndrome Congress and the Ronald McDonald McJobs program.

"I always wanted to be an actor," he said. "I always wanted to help the disabled. Now I'm doing both."

Through his efforts, Chris has changed the lives of disabled people around the country.

*Through his efforts, Chris has changed the lives
of disabled people around the country.*

Evidence of his good works appears in the mountains of letters he receives.

Chris's favorite letter came from a fan in Iowa. It reads:

Dear Chris,

I am 17 years old and I have Down syndrome just like you. You are my hero. You have changed my world.

Chris Burke is more than an amazing actor. He has become a true American hero.

CHRIS BURKE'S ADDRESS

You can write to Chris Burke at the following address:

Chris Burke
c/o Life Goes On
Warner Bros. TV
4000 Warner Boulevard
Burbank, CA 91505